One Defining Moment

One Defining Moment

How to Stay Happy and Balanced Amid a World Full of Undisclosed Energy…All It Takes Is a Breath

Written by Paula, Inspired by Lord Buddha

Foreword

No matter how spiritually expanded you become, there will be times when fear, frenzy, chaos, or paranoia creep into your thoughts. The world is overcrowded with turbulent overtones, and it is important to know these deterrents can drift in the recesses of your mind like computer pop-ups demanding attention. You needn't acquiesce though; the primary reason you perceive fearful energy is a boomerang effect of personal or planetary past moments in time. Whether this happening refers to minutes ago or lifetimes gone by, there is nothing to do. Each time a fearful thought attempts to set you off balance, exhale the worry and inhale with an idea of what you like to do most. Let the image restore peace, hold steadfast, and carry on.

Contents

Contents

Chapter 1
Maintaining Happiness

Along every pathway, there is duality. This natural facet of life in the third dimension enables you to experience periods of both light and dark within the same day. Everything was designed to express in opposites and was modeled after how Earth and human beings were created to be.

The geographic extremes seen in mountains versus deep valleys, the oceans versus vast deserts, and the Arctic Circle versus the equator, are other examples of opposite conditions constituting parts of the same globe, our magnificent planet. The patterning in human form is expressed as equal halves of female and male energy, constituting a whole person, as demonstrated in the yin and yang principle. Emotions may also appear to express in direct opposites, so there will be times when your emotional body feels elated and times when you're feeling deflated.

It may appear that you cannot have happy without sad, yet in this timing, when the planet and her inhabitants are gearing up for Ascension, I assure you there is another way. If happiness is the preferred way to be—and a person's highest choice for expression—then surely the power of intention makes way for being happy to linger and prevail. Happy can embrace sad moments and coddle them, as if they were only remnants of a story told long ago. Fear can be handled the same way, if you understand that the vibration creeps in from past sectors in time, making it futile to worry yourself. This most certainly will help balance any intense thoughts that have floated into your mental field.

Transpose any of these stray emotions by realizing you are a human being having a spiritual experience, which allows for everything, and takes into account the gift called *free will*, giving you an opportunity to either create or destroy. As one of God's children, you possess the natural right to dwell in a state of being that pleases you in every moment, so benefit from the idea of what brings you joy by envisioning it as part of your daily experience to manifest your reality.

In a state of peace, the only fight that may show up for the light warrior is a war waged with self. A battlefield full of dull thoughts as to why I am unhappy, why I am sad, why my life has to be full of disappointments, why love comes and goes, why? If you realize these little irreconcilable differences contain all the illusions you've ever held about yourself, clues may filter in to clarify how to shift them into compatible ideas.

An awakened being acknowledges that misconceptions may feel magnified at times, making them feel as if they are real. But the being also knows how to banish them from existence with a wave of an imaginary sword. This invisible weapon represents the recognition that some of what you experience comes from fearful false impressions, and this shrewd awareness helps slice through the density of forgotten memories and mass consciousness that can appear as a deceptive illusion or alternate reality.

Truth always comes in the quietude of being. A full breath in, followed by a long exhale, produces a moment of tranquility that helps to clarify thoughts and feelings that represent you, keeping you from haphazardly buying into those little energies that don't represent you. Use of this simple repetitive breathing sequence will establish the ability to decipher and know the difference. Chaos, panic, and apprehension all create shortness of breath that can lead to a multitude of unwanted physical symptoms caused by an inadequate amount of oxygen in your bloodstream.

When your breath is not choppy and you fully oxygenate, restoration of calm ushers in the remembrance that feelings of fear can drift in from anywhere, including past, present, future, past life memory, or mass consciousness, as it pertains to thought forms generated by human beings' basic survival efforts over time. It does not necessarily mean these thoughts hold any validity, if you are choosing trust, peace, and calm over calamity.

Forms of fear come in many varied adaptations, so to be able to hold fear, know it is fear, and then breathe your essence of love into it is a win-win, regardless of whether the energy sprang forth from outside you, or the energy generated itself from your own emotional and mental body. The reason I suggest you learn to identify the differential is to gain a greater sense of peace and reassurance in the drama of everyday life.

You may have what you would classify as a terrible day, and I can say that sometimes this happens because someone close to you may be having a terrible day, especially if it's connected to a person you'd been wishing and hoping would get his or her life in order. What you don't realize is that frame of mind actually makes you more prone to experiencing the same quality of feelings that the person journeys through. The primary lack of acceptance subjugates you to the same energy through the universal law of "what you resist persists."

You most likely are not choosing this at all, so there is great power in the ability to release any concern that someone close to you is in trouble or won't get it right. Move into the mind space of honoring everyone's choices as a divine and necessary part of their sojourn. By neutralizing judgments of something being good, bad, right, or wrong, you transmute restrictive energy for yourself and anyone else. In neutrality, you open a space of freedom to be and breathe, like welcoming sunlight as a smile from God.

The quality of life improves when you let nothing impair your state of being. No alternate reality, muddled illusions, or way of thinking can touch on your bliss unless you allow it, so if you become aware of energy filtering in that doesn't belong to you, kindly request that the angels uplift it. If you're dealing with your own unhappiness, then possibly you're engaging in belief systems that no longer suit you, indicating it might be time to let them fall to the ground like an old worn-out cape you've outgrown. Try on some new ideas for size and joyfully see what fits. Ideas may vary in color and shape just as quickly as a clothing change, so is it a fitting room or room for fitting?

Honoring this sacred balance by adding your own highest joy each time you participate in something that makes you feel happy triggers an immediate release of anything unhappy. The dismissal yields to peace and contentment, a natural segue into the *live and let live* adage, a way to maintain happiness!

Chapter 2
Clearing Energy

Daily doses of fresh air will revive and clear your energy field. For those of you who live in the city, this may be a challenge, but the rewards will far outweigh the time it takes to plan a short break. A little trip not far away from home can give a new perspective on an old matter. Relocating out of the vibration you dwell in daily can enliven your whole being with a sense of inspiration.

Energy can stagnate just like air, so the ancient practice of space clearing would behoove many. You could reorganize clothes, paperwork, and physical objects, or the clearing may be to sweep away arguments that have left behind unwanted clusters of lingering thought forms. Any space you spend any amount of time in will collect energy. Some may belong to you, others, or from mass consciousness, the collective brain of humankind whose thoughts permeate space and can leave the air feeling thick.

Native American brothers and sisters knew to burn dried-out sage as a way to clear discordant energy, similar to spraying air freshener in a room to give it cheer. These clearing efforts make way for new thoughts to enter; otherwise, the old monotonous ideas continue to get recycled and hang out in the space cluttering the mind with repeats. If you are choosing to generate steam and motion for fresh ways of living, an environmental cleanup of emotion is highly recommended. If this is not possible with sage or incense, you could always light a candle with a simple prayer on the flame to embrace unhelpful energy, so that you may start anew.

You could also accomplish this with a singing bowl, chimes, or any other way to produce a resonant sound, such as the blaring high note of a trumpet to move energy. Many people employ modern-day music as a way to give themselves an energy lift without ever consciously knowing that is what they're doing. Sound creates vibration and affects the whole being, so you can usefully apply these natural principles and universal laws regarding energy at any time.

Viewing that much of what you experience in life actually stems from the influence of unseen forces will help you employ "moving energy" techniques and avoid lengthy stagnation periods. Learning to handle stressful energies will empower you to reign supreme over challenging times by finding a new way to deal with any problematic development.

Let no troublesome situation linger in your space any longer than necessary to get your attention. No need to say, "Oh, this is horrible, and I cannot believe this is happening to me." Instead, rephrase with, "Oh, there are misaligned vibrations all around. How might I shift this energy and replace it with joy?" If the noise is not directly or consciously initiated by you to purposefully move energy, then it remains a static occupant, only adding more litter to the space. This is what happens when someone turns on a radio or television and utilizes the background noise as a form of companionship.

Next time you'd like to change the mood in a room, use the intonation of your voice coupled with a strong intention to do so, and witness the magic of transformation before your very senses! Your voice produces frequencies through tone and pitch that either move or create more energy, depending on what your voice is being used for. Whether you choose a full sentence, half sentence, one word, a laugh, or just hum, remember the combination of sound and your clearly formulated directive to shape shift energy is the stimulus for change.

Someone who hums or sings right after engaging in a heated argument may seem arrogant or indifferent, and yet the thought the person transmits is, "I refuse to let this get the better of me." The expressed intention through the combination of thought and sound is the subtle command that clears the argumentative energy. It's a way to shift the exchange of combative words into a neutral zone. What the other person does within the experience is up to him or her.

There will always be a choice about how to handle any demanding conversation. Some people will not be able to respond if they lack the confidence to reply in a way that matches exactly how they feel. So instead of even trying, they turn the frustration inward in forms of self-destructive behaviors. Others use the defense mechanism of simply tuning out another person's voice; genuine sharing through verbal communication may not be possible. Rather than endure the frustration of feeling your words bounce off a wall, you could go ahead and send thoughts via mental telepathy. Your own intention to create the space, surroundings, and atmosphere you choose to be in is what matters most, so utilizing thought transference affords you the satisfaction to get your point across no matter what.

Always remember a defensive move doesn't automatically warrant an offensive posture. No one can push your buttons unless you provide the power to do so. On the broad walk of life, if you choose to stay peaceful, then that mind space is where you will indeed remain. To the outside observer, it may seem you're oblivious to provocation, when in truth, it's just your simple choice to hold steadfast the energy field around you in order to stay calm. It takes much energy to fight back, especially if you feel the need to seek revenge. Then, you only end up matching hostility with more hostility. It's why you will notice people who fight their way through life look so worn out—it's exhausting! It is not the nature of *soul* to fight; it's the personality's need to defend itself.

Overcoming the lesser desire to retaliate is food for soul, as energies will not get caught up in a battle to make a delivery that is not based on love. Therefore, you lose none of your vital chi, and you remain full of the love and peace that created you to be. A spiritual warrior on the awakened pathway knows that radiating inner bliss is the closest way to become Godlike themselves. In a state of ecstasy, the only condition that exists is joy, allowing you to coexist with anything else and still maintain the heaven you create on earth.

Anything else might include anger, chaos, hostility, greed, betrayal, and any other fearful facets of being human that have survived time. You are aware of them, only they do not touch on your freedom or emotional body. As far as you're concerned, they are nonexistent, so you contribute nothing to their livelihood by adding more emotional fuel to promote their continued regeneration.

In actuality, the radiation of joy stops many aggressive thought forms in their tracks, and many retire or cease to exist after feeling such love and acceptance. Much different than the person who is already angry coming into contact with other angry thought forms and choosing to engage, this only generates more sine waves of the same by allowing additional anger to encircle the planet and proliferate, creating hell on earth.

At this juncture, I might add the question, "Whose anger is it?" Determining the answer will help you stop being a reactor or needing to entertain every motion of energy that drifts into your aura. This self-awareness brings an inner knowing on whether a charge of energy is coming from self or from an outside entity, person, place, group, or thing. Either way, having the willingness to calm antagonistic energy nurtures personal well-being and planetary peace.

From a worldly view, these exchanges go on millions and millions of times each day, and one less angry vibe makes a difference. It matters that one human being is out there who has the consciousness to arrest energy that does not flow in unconditional love. What a clearing that is!

Chapter 3
Caressing Candor

Candor is a form of freedom known to some as outspokenness. Thoughts and ideas expressed with candor complement a free-flowing lifestyle that keeps your aura and personal space clean; there is no delusion or deception to muddle through. Even though invisible, the resonance of truth vibrates like an echo, as it softly repeats and then gently fades away. Nothing in terms of unexpressed energy lingers. There is no need to clear energy or mentally reenact a conversation repeatedly to figure out what was said, and if it adequately represented what you really wanted to say, leaving you feeling tired out from the retracing of moments already passed.

Whether another agrees or disagrees is not what someone will remember. It's the flow of freedom gushing forth from having the courage to speak your truth that will leave an impression. It doesn't happen that often. A person is more accustomed to conversation that masks or protects the one speaking, and that only leaves question marks, since many times, what you hear doesn't match the feeling being transmitted. Speaking candidly gives others the confidence to know exactly where they stand with you. Little energy is wasted attempting to decode the subtle undertones that can persist long after the actual words are spoken, as you try to figure out why a person said what he or she said.

You can caress candor to suit your needs and customize how you choose to share it, so you need not deliver the words with a blunt-force blow. Think of your truth, or what you wish to express directly, by giving it a gentle stroke of approval, kindness, and love, and then watch how it falls from your lips. There is no power greater, as you add poignancy to what is verbalized and optimize the best way to effectively get your point across.

In terms of assisting humanity to be amenable to other points of view, a level of creative mastery is required for the development of a communication technique that will succeed in opening the heart and mind of the receiver. In general conversation, it may not seem quite as important as the instances when you hope to share something that could dramatically shift a person's perspective on life, thus giving the person a reprieve from stress and suffering. Big and small alike will respond to any charm or humor you add to the intention of speaking authentically without sugarcoating the meaning.

Each of you comprises both male and female energies. The masculine aspect initiates the desire to speak, and the feminine prepares the words as one would tender a gourmet meal. Together they form a union unparalleled by any other way of delivering a message. Caressing candor is a feat for the fittest. This savvy comes from experience and knowledge that to bombard people with your opinion may bring up their argumentative nature; hence, stifles prospects for a meaningful conversation.

The basic understanding that individuals will express personality preferences based on their own passionate theory of life alleviates any inclination to react with opinionated feedback, especially for those of you who are choosing to convey a message of healing by remaining neutral. Even though you may have the heartfelt urge to see other human beings address their character flaws (for the betterment of all and the planet), you'd best take a breath before falling into the trap of using specific topics like bullets at a firing range. See it instead as open ground, a space to penetrate energy fields of fight and fear with fair, by allowing them to carry on as long as they like about their topics of choice.

Listening quietly, even if you don't agree with any of what's said, may create an opening for them to hear another viewpoint, since there's no disagreement banter to distract them from their agenda. In tolerating their opinion, you let them get so caught up on the platform to ramble, that when you ask them to clarify exactly how their theory works, they may snap out of it when they realize they cannot give you an answer that makes sense. This personality rant may help them discover their own prejudice or fear, and that is how you use them as the target, rather than them making you the target.

If, for example, someone is going on and on about why they don't like people with a different skin color, the energy is already convoluted and will get sticky like minute threads of silk tangled in a spider's web, making it difficult even for the weaver of such a mess to untangle. They may not have ever had such an experience to recognize they've been placing belief in something that has ultimately alienated them from their own God-self, and the rest of the world. Spending time in fight mode to defend prejudicial stances keeps many from feeling the parameters of their biased opinions, so bless any of you for the gift of holding conversational space for them.

Caress candor by capitulating communication that represents who you are, and perhaps in the practice, set others free to BE too.

Chapter 4
Standing Offers

You experience many delicate lines in communication with others. Some of these margins appear when an offer is presented that awaits your decision. During this time, you'll have an opportunity to accept or decline, although taking the "think about it" option if uncertain gives you some time and space to mull it over.

If an offer brings a feeling of joy, your only task, other than agreeing to accept, is to be reassured by the happiness activated within you. This will help curtail any fear that creeps in when the mind takes over and starts to dissect every detail bit by bit, wanting to make sure you've done the right thing. Your mind as an individual component seeks only to protect you after all, so this is not shared to minimize the mental process. It is suggested to highlight the importance of considering how your body and spirit feel in the decision-making process, too. Taking the body, mind, and spirit into consideration optimizes your potential for great health and happiness, as you recognize in totality being a blend of all three.

If you decline an offer, but the situation starts to nag you by repeatedly coming back into your thoughts, perhaps a time of reflection is necessary. Any fear you uncover while contemplating can always be rectified with a future yes, granted the arrangement is still available. Once you amend your answer to the offer, you'll happily realign yourself, understanding a fear-based motive initially compelled you to say no.

If you need to analyze the proposal further, you might try writing down your thoughts and feelings in one of two columns, either *fear* or *fact*, and then take heed of the results. If most of your reasoning falls onto the fear side, do reconsider. If the decline was based mostly on facts that support your highest good, refresh yourself with the reminder, and just let it go.

This process of evaluating choices nurtures optimum conditions for further abundance to flow your way, because it keeps the energy field that encircles you open and clear for receiving. The self-maintenance is to ensure that future possibilities are not impeded in the energy of stagnation, either from letting an offer stand too long, or from not giving it proper recognition as a valuable prospect. Universal law responds to your efforts to sustain integrity and is an advocate of your prosperity, so never a reason to feel forlorn if you let an offer slip by. It's important to remember that there is an unlimited supply of abundance along with an assortment of creative ways future opportunities may be presented to you.

The important thing to remember is that if an offer produces a vibratory exhilaration that creates a physical reaction of humming or buzzing in your body, this definitely denotes a yes answer. Let it overrule any confusion. Trust the initial excitement generated as a guidepost to hold steadfast, rather than focus on trivial bits that may not be to your full liking. The moral of the story is to trust your body's response, knowing the creative Universe will also add its voice of support by producing unexpected synchronicities that may pleasantly adjust any small problematic details in a myriad of ways.

Never underestimate the raw production of happiness flooding your chakras, as the outpouring of whirling happy energy magnetically draws back more of the same. Like someone on a winning streak in Vegas, shrieks of delight accompany being on a roll of successive wins, as the basic premise of excitement keeps turning over more winning and excitement. Conversely, adverse effects on the body physical, such as feeling fatigued or worn out, will appear when conditions are not in your best interest, thus confirming a no answer.

The same type of drain can occur for those who feel comfortable only being on the giving end of life. The lack of balance as receivers leaves people prone to overextending themselves regarding the amount of time, money, and energy they realistically have to give, but they proceed anyway, believing it's the only way to get what they need. The expectation factor is out of sync too. Not realizing their proposal is driven by insecurity and a pseudo feeling of control, they may unconsciously demand more from others than they are able to clearly specify upfront, so everyone feels dissatisfied or insecure on both ends of an out-of-balance offer.

Similar misalignment configures when offers that don't feel right from the gate are accepted anyway out of fear that nothing else will come along. Once again, the main worry is about not having enough, so no one bothers to evaluate or negotiate. Both scenarios remain off kilter since they reflect lack of trust in an abundant Universe.

In conclusion, both the opening to make or receive an offer affords you ways to know yourself better. Nirvana is achieved when self-punishment, self-minimizing, and the tendencies toward martyrdom become nonexistent. In remembrance of your God-Given sovereign rights to create your own highest joy every moment, soul dwells in the enlightenment of bliss and freedom.

Nirvana is my standing offer to each of you, only I have no time constraint;   the   offer   is   good   for   eternity.

Chapter 5
Brief Encounters

Many days may pass before you think again about meeting up with someone momentarily. In the rush of a busy day, a brief exchange could be ultimately more meaningful than spending an entire lifetime with someone. As human beings going about your daily activities, you've got plenty on your mind regarding what needs to get accomplished. Even on a relaxed day, most of you will recycle thoughts and ideas frequently, keeping your mental body preoccupied. In this state of being, it is difficult to infuse the action-packed mind with a new suggestion or guidance.

Note: a passerby may make a life-changing comment. As your guides and guardians, we find many ways to get your attention. "Drop-ins," you could say. Even though we influence you from the nonphysical realm of being, many of us have also been on the planet at some point in our evolution and have the understanding of what it is like to walk in your shoes. As masters in the ascended state, we come and go as we choose, and that may include making appearances on Earth in a physical body for several minutes, or an extended amount of time if so impressed.

We dearly love humanity, and we will either take human form ourselves as a way to bring assistance or give someone else a nonphysical nudge to deliver a message we wish to impart. In the case of masters manifesting on Earth, we will take on a very ordinary appearance to blend into the general background with ease, so as not to frighten or startle you in any way. In the case of another person being the message bearer, it could be someone very close to you or a complete stranger.

You may think aloud about having met someone like this and say, "That was strange." Yes, most likely it was in the sense that the few words exchanged in the short meeting seemed way out of the ordinary for your logical mind to grasp. The same feeling may occur when someone you know spits out a few words that sound odd or way out of range for how they'd normally speak, but poignant at the same time. Spirit in play, friends!

Get the most out of your life by being aware of your surroundings at all times. Pay attention to people who show up mysteriously, and then vanish just as quickly. This could be one of God's special messengers sent to deliver some remarkable message through a glance, with a few words, or a quick point to a specific direction. Please don't chastise yourself if you feel you missed something or weren't able to connect the dots until days later. Again, if it is important, we will make sure that it is repeated until fully received by you!

The philosophy of only one chance to get it right doesn't exist for an ascended master, nor does a punishing God concept govern. We don't look down and think you're foolish if you didn't figure out the person tapping your shoulder to ask for directions was an Angel! We are patient, knowing the complexities of entertaining a body, mind, and spirit, especially since any one aspect of the trinity could engage you so completely on any given day, it might seem like a huge undertaking just to notice anything else.

Dedicated self-care is indeed a full-time job; however, if you realize you are already everything you hope to be, it occurs with no deed at all. A single breath activates this memory by simply adding conscious thought. The notion that you can become what you wish to be by merely breathing is quite a concept, especially when prior to that, you figured it would take incredible hard work and discipline on your part. The belief that it takes effort is only that, a belief. This particular idea, mocked-up over lifetimes, can also be just as easily simplified.

Breathing is the tool, as you inhale everything you prefer, and gently exhale or move with your breath whatever you choose to release. For instance, if you have a mental picture of an outcome or scenario that produces fear, erase it by exhaling the energy, and inhale a replacement image that inspires trust, peace, and calm.

A similar exercise can be applied to banish anxious thoughts or worrisome ideas. Just envision dusting off as you would a piece of furniture, and then conjure up a thought of shiny perfection and wellness to give yourself a polish. It is a form of mental fêng shui, only rather than dealing with the placement of objects in an external setting, the focus is on keeping your internal pathways unobstructed so that blood, energy, and oxygen flow freely to every part of your human body.

If you have a day when stagnant energy is depressing you to the point that you feel as though you are walking through glue, conduct a checkup. Taking a deep breath to quiet yourself is first, so when you feel stressed and frenzied but are aware it's not your energy, you can shape shift it into calmness by breathing in the chaos or discordant energy, and then exhale it as stillness.

You are a creator and have the power to transform anything. Similar to lighting sage or incense to clear a room that reeks of an unpleasant download of words emitting anger, you can also walk into disagreeable places or with persons who feel upsetting, and then move energy by making the choice to walk in tranquility. Through the process of inhalation, and then just as quickly breathing out by directing your attention on this breathing quality control, you become a great neutralizing breathalyzer.

The conscious thought you apply acts as your watchtower and guiding light, so release any concern that breathing in energetic disturbance can harm you. The energy you breathe in is the alchemical way to transmute it by allowing it to touch on a still point (the love of you), so that when it is released through exhaling, it has been balanced and returns to the environment as a clear vibration. You may not think such a simple procedure, taking only seconds to accomplish, could do any good in the big wide world around you, so I'd like to restore confidence by mentioning that, seen from our perspective, it does!

As you take in a breath of fear, and then knowingly breathe it back out as love, many will benefit. Perhaps you will not see any visible results, yet understand that every wave of peace delivers one less person hurt at the hand of another, one less unkind word getting unleashed, one less animal brutalized by a human being's hostility, or one less piece of trash thrown on Gaia.

Dearly beloved, the magic of your love bows before any beast, and merciful kindness will allay the motion of foul moods. Likened to the same way you would caress candor, where in the stroking, provoked energy is soothed. Know this, and as you bestow such a blessing upon the world, take the next moment to bless yourself. Adequate time has been given to saying, "God Bless You." Bring it full circle and complete by saying, "God Bless Me, Too."

The practice of personal spiritual housekeeping weaves automatically into a planetary sweep, because as you train yourself to recognize and deal with thoughts, ideas, or mental pictures that are fear based, you become a transformer for the world by transmuting energy. As an awakened being, it opens-up an all-encompassing awareness of the ways people suffer, and the realization to blend unseen energy dynamics into one with the all, and all with the one.

At the end of the day, you will have no need to distinguish whether energy is personal or planetary, since your primary objective is to facilitate peace it all goes into the same blender of love anyway. This is the way of the bodhisattva, a disciplined light warrior trained to handle any onslaught of energetic warfare. The application of breath dedicated to "love's name" creates for the disciple wholeness and union with divine providence, whereby they become a medium for all of humanity to receive a similar proxy, immediately aligning any notion that selflessness is more dignified than the autonomy that comes from being self-satisfied.

Finally, a brush with hostility can either ruin your day as you fall into a murky swamp of energy that influences everything you do and say, or on the other hand, keep any unpleasant experience short-lived by remembering that feelings of fear or anger can be aligned in a single breath. It's the moment it takes to direct this awareness as you inhale "In you go, fear," as if you're a magical oven, and the heat of you fires it into love on the next exhale.

I know it may seem hard to believe, especially when many light-workers have let out a sigh at the amount of anger and aggression expressed in the world, and they feel hopeless to know how to possibly balance that which has spiraled out of control. One breath at a time, dear ones, is how to align any misgiving and keep it a brief encounter.

Chapter 6

Minutes Can Turn Back the Hands of Time

In an effort to save humanity from prolonged unnecessary suffering, I share the reminder of how quickly any given set of circumstances can change. A matter of minutes can unveil devastating weather conditions or produce waves of heartache caused from words carelessly spoken, but those same decisive moments can also glorify one through the joy that comes from the flow of divine intervention and dreams come true.

In the latter situation, all previous disharmonies seem to melt away with the arrival of an unexpected gift of love, beauty, or abundance. Any previous dissatisfaction gets magically embraced in a split second, like the first kiss of morning sunlight upon the darkened land, diminishing gloomy like it never existed.

I encourage you to entertain this spark each day as you go about your tasks, perhaps creating new ones especially designed for this express purpose. Some lovely visual representation of dreams come true upon an altar you can cherish whenever you look that way. Each time you add a pleasing thought or vision to those currents of energy, it's like tossing a magnetic charm into your life stream. Flowing like a river, it will twist, turn, and splash over any obstacles in a targeted effort to collect any ingredients that add gusto to the manifestation of your heart wish.

You are magnificent creators, and I encourage you to remember that a single wish or thought is never lost, but continually reproduces itself in the livelihood of ideas you create. Without faith in a higher power co-creatively overseeing your lives based on what you've chosen to experience, very little hope remains.

The same holds true for your ability to calm stormy waters. If your river (life course) gets rough and choppy, please add peace and calm until each thought and suggestion added restores the current to placid. No one has the authority to alter your life stream unless you give permission to do so.

If, for example, someone throws something in your river that is not pleasant, like vulgar thoughts or actions, then it is your responsibility to rid your river of the pollution. It is your job to identify where it has been strewn about, and fish it out! A general feeling of malaise, along with unusual aches and pains in your physical body may provide the clue that something like this has occurred.

In the reverse, if you gain permission to be a contributor in other lives, you are responsible for what you put into their streams. Nothing goes unnoticed by the Godhead, so even though someone gave you access doesn't mean that the quality of what you throw in will not be surveyed. All of it must add up to honoring if it is to be in accord and harmony with Universal Law.

If you have deliberately dishonored another human being, most likely it is because you dishonor yourself. Knowing this, we take into account the learning curve. If you become aware that you have thrown an unhelpful thought into another's river, you do yourself a great service to fetch it out and reclaim it as your own since you were the creator of it. You can neutralize it by breathing in the disparaging thought on the inhalation, and then breathing it out on the exhale as an invisible light into the palm of your hand as you "cancel clear" the energy of it with your mind and breath.

The conscious act of retrieving one unkind thought is enough to clean up any stream involved with the purity of light and love. This awakens you to the prospect of any other time you may have done the same, and recall having thoughts that were hurtful or punishing to another being. Several vicious thoughts thrown into a river can rouse a wake, just as several loving thoughts can restore stillness, so the activity depends on your involvement, which you are accountable for either way. My objective is for you to understand the tossing of a gentle rose petal or a rock pelted in to stir are both actions that register on your own chartered journey.

We in the ascended state, having already overcome some of the same hurdles when in human form, understand the process and have no reason to judge. We hold space for more to awaken so that energies can be transformed individually until all rivers (all lives/life streams) flow in mutual love and respect, encompassing the planet in gentleness. I give you the idea of the river so that you may also understand the great influence your *life stream story* has on earth.

You can redo anything if need be, for just as you have the ability to destroy, you have the same irrevocable power to create. Think of what you can do or completely undo in a matter of minutes. A precautionary tool would involve being cognizant of the thoughts you have regarding yourself and others. This suggestion will help you notice that many times the thoughts you have about yourself are very similar in tone and content to the ones you have about others; they just get projected outward. Inner peace is derived from self-love, and if self-love lacks, it will be expressed in an assortment of fear-based ways.

This summing up of personal data is my strongest case for achieving lasting peace. Then at the end of each day, when you turn in, you can take comfort in the satisfaction of knowing you have not damaged yourself in any way through uncomplimentary self-imposed influences that likewise may have hurt others by unchecked thoughts you've sent out. Once fully aware they exist and repeat, you are in a greater position to retire them if they are generated from your own mind, or return thought forms to their source, if they belong elsewhere.

I empower you to hold the hands of time favorably through the clean living that comes from taking full responsibility for yourself, and as a compliment to God and to your God-self, rightfully maximize the power of creation within you to fill your reality with highest joy in every moment!

Chapter 7

Being

When you hold no stake in the outcome of things, you are being. If you are more concerned whether something happens or doesn't happen, your energies are invested, so you're only efforting to BE. When what will be, or not be, both hold the same value in terms of outcomes, you are in a state of *beingness*. This means you have defused the definitions of emotion-packed terms like positive, negative, glory, disaster, death, birth, marriage, and divorce, recognizing one is neither greater nor less than the other, and in equalization you achieve karma for dharma.

No longer will your causal body entertain propensities that formerly exhausted your adrenals in the push-pull exertion of striving for something on account of desire. In honoring all that is, you are able to hold and preserve your essence so that your energy field remains stable and unwavering, thereby creating a holding tank of personal power to garner from for manifesting what, where, and when you choose.

In the freedom of neutrality, any amped-up energy approaching your aura will simply recoil and bounce back to the source, since there was no magnetic draw from your own emotional body to anchor it. From this place of impartiality, there is no need for the body-mind-spirit unit to collect any frequency that doesn't represent its God-Given "I Am" form, which steadfastly remains unaltered by anyone or anything. "I Am" is soul essence in its entirety, including your past, present, and future. The timeless light-body energy distinctly represents who you are.

One who is operating in a state of beingness may appear to others as grossly disconnected from life's pertinent matters. Having neutralized bias and partiality from their thought process, they have no pronounced opinions, so another person may perceive it as not caring or having a lack of interest in societal standards of living.

This determination is made because folk haven't registered that it's a place of nonjudgment not fueled by emotion they are sensing, so most wouldn't recognize it as the divinity of beingness, having never achieved such status themselves.

When you can allow for the good, the bad, the right, the wrong, the rich, or the poor, and consider no one situation grander than the other, it is mastery! This indicates you have learned your lessons on Earth. When you have overcome repeated episodes in life designed to stir you, but they stir you no more, you know you've graduated, and the need to reincarnate ceases to exist. Since you've collected all there is to learn based on what you came to experience, the need for further incarnations in human form is no longer necessary.

The accomplishment of personal lessons learned transition into an energetic impetus for anyone else choosing to self-examine, and the awareness becomes available as an offering to the rest of the world like starlight. These frequencies of inspiration and victory reach out like a simultaneous broadcast, and anyone else who is wishing to grow and expand captures them. Even though invisible, this wave of progressive energy is obtainable because of your divine connectedness to each other as children of the same God.

All subconscious minds are connected accordingly, and so unseen events like this are a great reflection of the phrase, *one for all,* and *all for one.*

How long a lesson repeats or drags on for anyone else is of no consequence to you. Having removed the need to judge from your mental inclinations is the focal point, for the reason that it honors each being's unique development and whatever repertoire may be included as a necessary part of the journey.

To sum up, you are detached even though still attached, just not emotionally bound in any way. This is the mastery of being. Oneness embracing eternity is the result and a glimpse of how life everlasting might feel. As you surrender to this stillness, you may wonder if it's OK to be so calm. This most likely is owing to chaos and frenzy still feeling more familiar to you, so rather than claim the bliss that comes from a peaceful existence, it might feel easier to adopt depression and live by seemingly lackluster definitions instead.

These feelings won't spiral out of control if you can pause long enough to stop comparing your state of being to anyone else's process. If you realize it's OK to accept that all you have ever longed for was the permission to just BE, without worry, then tranquility is what will ensue. The comparison factor is something many relate to and participate in—not realizing the analyzing is actually how you depress yourself. All that matters is being aware of when your thinking leans that way so you can make a different choice if you feel complete with competition and drama. There is nothing to live up to then, and no reason to feel let down.

Days of peace and meditation will lead to your spiritual abilities opening, and you may have moments of acute knowing, synchronicities, and unusual psychic occurrences. This results from spiritual practice that triggers and activates your God/Goddess higher self, so there is no need to attribute these happenings to some other outside stimuli. Fortune tellers speak of luck and superstition; however, a master will reflect the control and discipline it takes to rein in the authority for manifesting miracles.

You are so accustomed to accepting that such gifts are not within the scope of your own capabilities, that the idea of having the power as a creator to mold and shape the reality you live in just doesn't compute. Much time within evolution has been spent studying the mechanics of life via science, theory, and philosophy. You've needed to investigate how things work and why, so when little unseen awakenings occur within, the first thing you do is to grasp for what it means via your mental faculty. Looking for an explanation via black-and-white proof minimizes the particular meaning these occurrences may have as part of your own unique spiritual involution.

Evolution is the developmental process of the body from the beginning of physical form until the present time. Involution is the inward process of each being's life stream energy from the inception of its essence (soul) in a body until this moment and onward. Evolution of the human form comes to completion when a person ascends; involution continues for eternity. If you are choosing to ascend, your *physical* body will continue to evolve until all cellular structures resonate to your higher God Self, ascending your physical presence into a full *light* body of soul essence. This grand transformation occurs as a gradual shapeshifting, likened to the metamorphosis of a pupa one day transitioning into a butterfly.

Let me elucidate. As you adjust to being, you can float around, too! Once you realize you don't have to DO in order to BE, you can just enjoy how it feels being, also similar to what existence feels like in the outer realms or what you refer to as the "other side." In both situations, time is inconsequential, resulting in an ease of being, complemented by a lack of pressure to accomplish or do something.

This level of acceptance and self-worth embodies the art of mastering human form. You can just Be, until something comes along that requires action or doing on your part, and in that moment make a decision on what to do, according to how it flows with being. This could include anything from reaching out to make a phone call to following through with an urge to do the dishes.

So, in being, there is no plan or course of action. There is moment-to-moment trust of your natural inclinations and the knowledge that you don't need to push to get things done. Quite different from when you walk around from morning till night, planning things out in your head on how things should go and when and where they will take place. This is not being; it is supervising.

Once you acclimate to the peace of beingness, you may worry about getting swallowed up in an empty void of sheer nothingness from being so still. Even though it may feel that way, there is no need to worry. You are sensing the endless nature of eternity and experiencing what a never-ending existence might feel like. It is a part of your birthright to feel the freedom of infinity while still encapsulated in human form, although you may prefer waiting till falling asleep to test the waters of unlimitedness when you naturally exit without thought or effort.

You are pure energy and not stuck inside the body never to leave it, as validated through your ability to roam about freely in dreamtime. The premise of beingness incorporates the same principle while awake, because you can move in or out of the body just as easily, especially with applied conscious thought to the fact that you can. If you know when you are daydreaming about being elsewhere, that in fact you are being elsewhere, it becomes a self-confirming journey, and not just an extraneous exercise meant only to pass time away. Without the application of conscious thought and movement, the daydreaming experience is left to be defined only as a hazy happenstance dream.

The discussion is mostly for you to know you can experience the unlimited scope of existence even though you dwell in the energy of limitedness. (The human body and scientific knowledge as it relates to three-dimensional existence, time, and space.) This illuminating concept also suggests oneness for the polarities of day and night. You might say, "But it is dark at night and not dark during the day." I would say that during the day, if you close your eyes, you'll see dark. During the evening, if you look to the sky, there is the light, thus dispelling the illusion that daytime is separate from nighttime.

You learn the urge to compartmentalize at an early age, so a tendency to site distinction prevails. My promissory note is that the threads of existence all weave together anyway. Is it a fragment of your imagination if you dream when asleep, or dream while awake? You are still dreaming, especially in light of the fact that your spiritual nature allows you to move in and out of the body without restriction in either state.

Thoughts of another duality collect in the question "Can you ever really be physically alone?" Yes and no. You can be with people and still feel alone, or you can be physically alone and not feel alone at all. A lack of judgment causes the latter to happen, in that you've created no separation—you've put no barriers between you and anything or anyone else. You are completely alone, and completely not alone, feeling the camaraderie of everyone (the outside world) within you.

The times when you are alone and imagining what it would be like to be with someone, are actually you being and embracing that aspect of humanity. In your aloneness, you can unite with a woman or man on her or his wedding day as if it were your own. You can merge with the family playing in the park, or you can be enjoying a group of friends' company in someone's home. You are able to imagine it, because you already are part of it. The union is so full, it may teeter over at times to an alone feeling until you adjust your energy to the frequency of being one with the all, and all with the one…it equals one you encircling all that is.

What I have been choosing to impart, is that whether you are alone or surrounded by friends and family, it is equivalent. You all have been participating in these experiences throughout time, therefore, they are a part of you, and you are a part of them. You are not separate from anything but interconnected to everything!

All opposite conditions were created for finding a place in the middle that shows no favoritism to either side. The goal is to merge, meet, and become one. For instance, sad merged with glad is the fullness of sadness, and the fullness of gladness in equal parts, so in the blending, it would be hard to imagine one being less than or greater than the other. Having experienced both the fullness of sadness and gladness helps to conceptualize that in wholeness, they are equal. A simple example would be that you can burst into a tearful, heartfelt cry over feeling pure joy, but also fall into a sob over feeling deep grief and paralyzing sadness. The equality in both differentials is demonstrated through the elementary expression of each being the same.

All such extremes in human emotion will feel less disturbing by allowing them to simply be what they are, and understanding that energy seeks only to be acknowledged. You can see it more from a systematic point of view by responding to emotion rather than reacting. It's possible to accomplish this task by holding yourself steadfast in all situations. Any emotion will balance when embraced in the tenacious calm of acceptance, extinguishing the need to replicate for attention, and receive an immediate reprieve instead.

The grandest gift you could bestow upon any energy is the unwavering peace of your eternal soul. A state of being that exemplifies you can reside within the drama, trauma, and frenzy of each day, knowing it is all a part of what human beings are choosing to express, without feeling like you must alter yourself to accommodate it all. "It is what it is" philosophy will help keep the focus on maintaining a neutral position where nothing provokes you to step out of your center point.

If you can imagine the amount of emotion generated over the eons of time human form has been in existence, you would get the picture of how it has layered itself around the earth's stratosphere like thick rubber bands pulsating each time they're engaged. When someone experiences a strong emotion, it pulls upon these corresponding bands of energy, whereby more of the same motion gets reactivated as it vibrates outwardly to the masses and pummels the earth with its reverberatory sensations.

Imagine the calm enlisted each time you choose not to be reactive, but instead focus on being and breathing to still these ripples of emotional energy. Each precious meditative moment adds to creating a suitable atmosphere so Gaia can restore herself, in place of expending the fullness of vitality just to sustain her physical form. She is supported to hold steadfast amid the pounding gyrations of warring energies that threaten to implode her into a million bits and pieces as they reverberate to her core. As some of you awaken and prefer tranquility to chaos, she is able to hold some energy in reserve for healing her wounds.

Gaia, reclaiming the pristine condition of her birth from the beginning of time is a grand vision to behold *chelas* (pupil), made anew, like one choosing to Ascend.

Chapter 8

Green, the Undeniable Motion of Planet Earth

Earth's essence has been superimposed with a megahertz that vibrates to the color green, and everything on the planet ultimately becomes restored to green no matter the devastation that sweeps over an area. The cellular structures within every microcosm/macrocosm of every living thing have been imbued with the power to regenerate. If this concept is applied to the idea of your own involution/evolution, the regeneration called hope that nurtures the in-process parts of yourself will flow continually.

When you experience some form of wreckage in your daily lives, you have a tendency to beat yourself up or sink into depression as it ignites thoughts of failure, wrongdoing, or poor judgment. Gaia does not judge after a fire sweeps across her surface; she simply repairs at the first chance to do so. The same happens when you take in a little nourishment in whatever form you are drawn to, such as food, sleep, water, walks, massage, rest, time alone, or time with friends, etc., and the self-recovery it brings.

The creator knew what human beings would muster with use of their free will and wanted to supply as many signposts along the way as possible. Nature models to you the cyclic events of repair as a way to constantly reflect you are capable of the same restoration. The green grass provides nutrients that indirectly feed the body, mind, and spirit in a variety of ways, so you can envision a similar blanket of color nourishing your whole being from the inside out. Fill your senses by rolling out this imaginary carpet of color after experiencing a good cry, illness, upset, or anger, and then picture the renovation.

It can serve as a great inspiration to remember the renewal that occurs after a fire blackens a piece of land. Green shoots sprout after a rainfall; shortly thereafter, the land dons a new cape of green. You can absolutely achieve the same results, if you fully believe that healing yourself through visualization is possible.

Respectively, if feeling bleak, you can instantly envision yourself being renewed by brilliant transmuting sunshine.

Go green, is a term used to represent healthy environmental conditions. The concept of recycling is paramount to Earth so that more trash doesn't build up and cause toxicity in the soil and air, not only affecting the quality of life for each individual, but also causing a disturbance in weather patterns. Being mindful of the earth's chakras/energy centers is essential because these orifices have become congested with deposits of waste, and the consequences are dire.

The same holds true for your physical body. Similar to a landfill, you can only take so much buildup before another location, organ, or system needs to be utilized when the old place starts to exhibit symptoms of disease and overuse. Minding yourself mentally, physically, and spiritually is a way to have control over your own atmospheric pressures and influences in order to maintain the motion of healthy chakras so you stay open and clear.

The next step is to consciously apply the same care and respect to Gaia by imagining greenery replacing all the trash, bright lights, stop signs, and cement. Picturing the globe blanketed in a carpet of green is a way to give Mother Earth a reformative thank-you for having supported your human form throughout time. She is in her own involution/evolution process, and this image of green peace promotes the undeniable motion of her own impending Ascension.

Chapter 9

When You Pay Your Whole Life Competing

If life is lived as a competition, what's left is an outcome of win, lose, or quit. Once you establish what it is you're competing for, it may be easier to discern if that's what you truly want, or if you just got swallowed up in the contest to gain, which engulfs many societies.

What is in flow for your daily life and the plans you make will show up as a natural burst of excitement if it warrants pursuing. This confirmation of positive energy being generated within your body springs forth from a place of joy. When an idea is not in flow, it will be followed by lethargy and fatigue induced from inner struggle, indicating no resonance for your highest good or pleasure. To keep it simple when making decisions, a vibration of excitement suggests a yes answer, and suddenly feeling exhausted signifies a no. It would serve each of you well to take note of the frequencies humming within your body as a way for inner self to communicate to you through your senses.

You may find something that brings enjoyment but subconsciously push it aside, as if you don't feel deserving or worthy of it. This observation seems to imply it is more comfortable to stick with tasks that don't contain much happiness, simply because that's what may be more familiar to you. To have the freedom of each day in the palm of your hand to do as you please feels like too much of a luxury to claim, and might be considered by some as over the top, selfish, or downright extravagant. These unforgiving thought forms have etched themselves in linear time through human beings' DNA. I suggest challenging these old memory links by paying closer attention to your body's physical responses and creating an exciting new life.

We understand it is easy enough to be immersed in the hoopla of mainstream society's billboard messages, world events, and the trauma of listening to the daily news alone! Even five minutes of quiet time can give you enough space to focus on your own feelings, so if there is an important decision to be made, you've ensured the best outcome regarding your well-being and happiness. It is easy to feel swept away by what others may deem as true and valid, but the real glory comes from the internal pursuit of self-knowledge.

You may even ask a simple question of yourself to determine where you are on the energy scale of feeling. For example, "How do I feel about what I do every day of my life?" You all understand what it felt like to be questioned on a quiz in school, but to ask yourself a question about self just doesn't come in as a normal urge to do so. Being aware and willing is all it takes.

When you find yourself feeling uncertain or confused, allow self-query to fill that mental space, and in quietude feel the matching corresponding vibration. The body, mind, spirit engine will never transmit false information, so you can trust the energy answer you receive. If there is no clear identifiable response, then continue to ask over a period until clarity arrives. Outside sources may attempt to dictate what your state of being should be, but your body, the vessel for soul's light, will never deliver a message other than truth about your core. It's well worth taking the time to be your own authority.

Know what you are competing for and whether it pleases you, because if it doesn't, then outside pressures are most likely what compel your every move. If an idea makes you happy, it will automatically complement your general state of being; whereas, if it stresses you out, it is most likely not so great for your well-being. My suggestion is to compete only for your own attention. There within is the glory for lasting happiness.

An example of being displeased is someone reaching his or her senior years with everything they could want in terms of financial security, yet unable to enjoy accrued abundance and the work it took to gain such stability because of an overall dissatisfaction and restlessness. A sure sign of someone who fell into the competition sweep and never escaped the dustpan. On the other hand, you may have heard about a hermit who lived alone somewhere in the hills and exclaimed, "What a lowly life to lead." The hermit may have felt inwardly very satisfied, happy, and peaceful, so who merits the authority to say other than the one living it?

There will always be the matter of having to make sense of decisions made in life that immediately access the mental body. It is more of a challenge to get in touch with how you are feeling when the mind is engaged, but this is not meant to undermine the incredible intrinsic value that logic can play, especially when various details need sorting to be certain your basic needs are met. Even though you may be more used to accessing the mind, you are encouraged to lead with your heart. No one can see this light go out, but I can guarantee it is a living thing, and its essence permeates even the deepest and darkest of impossible situations.

Sit not in a think tank then; rather, let your heart's wishes roll like torrents of a raging river, trusting the Universe notices the flow of every life stream and is interested in what is returned to you. See your heart-held dreams gushing forth like water breaking through a dam. Let this be the exercise you practice when your mental body tires you out, as in the case of the diligent thinker, corralling the same data continually, exercising an ability to repeat thoughts, but never coming up with cheerful solutions or results.

Much emphasis has been placed on 3-D and the importance of having a plan. Many times, planning works with satisfactory results; other times, even the best laid plans can start without a glitch, and then stagnate because of natural changes occurring day to day within a person's psyche, shifting the original pursuit completely. On a small scale, this might include canceling plans that felt perfect the night before, but upon waking, no longer felt in harmony. By allowing for these little reversals and subsequent shifts in plans, more and more joy will express until starting each day begins to feel fluid and hope-filled once again.

Nothing remains in a state of inertia or without motion, and like Earth, the energy emitted daily is oscillating and constantly revolving, so adding joyful intentions to your involution can only strengthen your ability to move freely about this Universe as you please. Be adept at knowing your heart wish energy spins like a top, and where it stops or lands, is exactly where it is meant to be.

Your atomic structures and cells renew themselves to reflect each thought, thus increasing the potential to manifest great health, visions, and dreams. Your body hears every word you think or say, and so the ideas you have about yourself determine how you will be. Repeating "I am the picture of eternal youth and beauty" on a daily basis produces an eternally youthful human being, beaming wellness from inside out. Conversely, if you say you are sick enough times with the strength of belief behind it, you will be sick. There is no superstition involved. It is the repeated directive that governs cellular integrity. A matching physical constitution is created as a byproduct of that engineering.

The power of soul is unlimited and doesn't give credit to words like terminal, poor, unlucky, sad, bad, depressed, etc. Soul awaits the most favorable time to unleash its influence and savors each moment, knowing eventually, the personality will exhaust its coping mechanism and the human being will turn inward. You might ask, "Why doesn't the soul just take over when the personality is wearing a person out? Why doesn't the soul just step in to remedy the situation?" The answer is because soul is unconditional love and honors the personality by allowing for the choices made to rule accordingly. This process could take under five minutes, or an entire lifetime before a person calls upon his or her soul.

A simple sign of soul stepping in may be an unusually long exhale followed by a distinct feeling of calm and resignation. You may recognize taking deeper breaths and realize in one divine moment that some marvelous shift has occurred within you!

Ah, food for thought, dear ones, a sharing on how to minimize feeling pressured or that you need to continue *competing to get ahead in life* if you are ready for a change. Go forth with thoughts that bring you happiness and create time to relax. This will provide an awareness to know whether you are operating in the energy of being or competing.

You are God's unique creation and therefore worthy of launching concepts, visualizations, and plans that keep you vibrating in the energy of joy. If various activities feel like a push or hard work, they most likely are not adding to a lifelong chant of personal contentment and freedom.

You were born into specific human conditions as an opportunity to be delivered from temptations to reside in personality-driven instincts and claim the sovereignty of living in soul. The personality aspect will push for immediate gratification; soul has the grace to wait until perfect conditions show up for an outcome that promotes your highest good and joy with ease.

The most worthwhile competition you'll ever participate in is the one where you strive to gain your own soul's attention.

Chapter 10
The Original Guilt

From the beginning of time, it has been suggested that somebody done somebody wrong, and it is the primary reason you carry the "original guilt." This complex is not only embedded in your DNA, but also groomed into every code of ethics recorded on planet Earth. Guilt is deeply etched in the consciousness of humankind. It has left an impression on the physical body by implanting itself in the skeletal structure of human beings.

The vertebrae carry memory of this burdensome belief that says you are not only responsible for yourself, but everyone else too. Since the spinal column bones link together to support and uphold the entire body, one false conviction can easily compromise a person's physical integrity. One is left hunched over with various forms of bone and muscle disease, such as arthritis, atrophy, degeneration, fibromyalgia, and any other illnesses that don't allow the body to function with ease or comfortably hold itself upright.

Implied in these conditions and faulty posture is the guilt of not being able to hold another person up or monitor the person's actions, reactions, and deeds. The body carries the weight of this failing, and then to add more shame, we ask ourselves, "Dare I pleasure myself or spend time supporting and looking after my own interests when others need help?" Various forms of depression and poor health are sure to follow.

Soul, I AM essence, is the only solution to any such irregularity, since the acknowledgment of this awakened state of being permits nothing to interfere with its form or energy. Once called upon, it is also capable of fully healing any former maladjustment or misalignment. The God-Given knowing that each being is entitled to the fullness of personal contentment, even though others may suffer, is the recommended belief to ensure making a potent I AM decree.

Whether you are energetically uplifting a single human being, an entire race, or a discriminatory belief structure, then yes, you might show the tendency to be chronically fatigued or hunched over from dealing with the extra weight on overtaxed muscles, bones, and joints. The joints, similar to the vertebra are connectors, and if flawed consciousness resides in the place being connected, then that discrepancy is carried to the connecting tissue and any surrounding accessory, such as the nervous system, muscles, or organs.

For this reason, it is most important to flush your system with the essence of light-filled thought, such as, *I AM deserving of a happy life lived in freedom*, superseding any former belief system, because it matches the divinity of God's unflawed image of you. This vision may feel distorted for those who still believe they are fully responsible to cure and fix other people in their life. You are only liable for your own actions, and there within is the best way to demonstrate how to live. In God's eye, leading by example is abundantly enough, but according to the guilt complex, it is never enough—even when you are crawling on your knees and begging.

The original sin led to the understanding that a person is totally accountable for coercing another person to join them in wrongdoing. It was really meant to show what can happen in any cocreation. Eve was depicted as the one responsible for man's downfall, and yet if the tables had been turned, it could have been any number of creative combinations to show the same thing, including Adam as the culprit. Cocreation means people are responsible for the decisions they make under major influence or no influence at all! The fact that Adam conceded to Eve's wishes was his part in the cocreation, shifting the destiny and consciousness of the human race in a dramatic way.

Essentially, free will was given to empower, not lessen who and what you are by saying, "Oh, I made a mistake and will suffer for that decision for the rest of my days!" It is not necessary to refer to a condescending and punishing frame of mind, if you know that learning from your mistakes is what softens guilt by using each slipup as a stepping-stone for personality quirks to align with the higher self. This concept, along with the understanding that there is more than one chance to get it right (lifetimes if needed) also helps to eradicate a guilty hangover.

If you don't believe you're entitled to be happy unless your partner, son, daughter, or friend is happy, then it equates to a lifetime of feeling less than and undeserving, for there will always be someone in your life whose choices have left them unhappy. Some believe God said, "Go and lift the heaviness of your brother." God said, "Be your brother, and in doing so lift much agony through compassion." (Lord Buddha) It's possible to have empathy without carrying a cross and show suffering to prove you care.

Our beloved Jesus meant to demonstrate one crucifixion was enough; nevertheless, humanity insists they must also mimic the cross-bearing journey, believing this is the only way to show God they are holy. No interpretation of holiness is any less than another, so if you feel the need to carry a cross, one day when the burden is too heavy, you may drop it out of exhaustion, and that is what actually may expand your beliefs on carrying it to begin with. If humanity does not address the original guilt, many will continue to feel awful about being laden with fault and shame, causing them to lash out and injure themselves or others.

Breathe in permission to exhale guilt and be all that you can be within the resonance of who you are. You were created in God's image as Gods and Goddesses, rather than only relegating the title to a select few who have proved worthiness by putting down their lives for others.

The new paradigm suggests there is no glory in self-sacrifice that is inspired by guilt; this is only a minimization of self. On the flip side, any self-sacrifice motivated out of pure love doesn't feel like duty, because it springs forth from the heart-centered love of a person, and the giving is like drinking from a self-replenishing fountain. The experience is created from a full cup, so you can give,

give, give, and the other person can take, take, take, and your energy level will not be depleted. Offering assistance from a half-full cup, mixed with obligation, will leave you feeling drained.

In lieu of the original guilt plaguing humanity by keeping many in the half-full/less than experience, we flood earth with unconditional love for the divine feminine to be pardoned from the haunting blame that infringes on her freedom. The heartfelt aim is for restoration of the feminine image so that it can be holy and fully embraced by every individual as an equal half of his or her whole being. Wholeness is a byproduct of happiness. It is what a person exudes when they have a cup full of peace and contentment.

Let every moment define worthiness of personal freedom and joy, then watch the course of your life change direction.